Scars Not Stones
Freedom From The Chains Of Your Past

Donna Williams

ISBN-10: 0692478930

ISBN-13: 978-0692478936

DEDICATION

I dedicate this book to the glory of God. Without His
outpouring, it would never have become a reality. It is
dedicated, also, to the ones for whom the Lord will use
this little book to break your chains and set you free. Run
hard after the Lord and all that He has for you.

ACKNOWLEDGEMENTS

Thank You, Lord, for entrusting this to me. Deepest
thanks to my husband, Jerry, for being one of my greatest
inspirations in the faith and my biggest cheerleader. To
the EPIC Board Members and our Alliance leadership
team for your faithful commitment to us. Your love and
support has been used of the Lord to bring strength to
our lives that is the stuff of Heaven. Thank you to
Richard White of Richard White Productions, Shreveport,
Louisiana, for the cover photo. Finally, I want thank all
those who were instruments of the Lord to teach me the
lessons I have learned that are shared within this book.

Donna Williams

CONTENTS

Preface

Do you have a past? Do you have things in your past that you are not proud of? Are you haunted by the fear that maybe someone will find out? This is one of the most significant areas in which the enemy attacks to try to keep us from stepping out into all that God has for us and becoming all that He has called us to be.

The fact is that everyone has a past and things therein of which they are not proud. I, too, have been plagued by the fear that someone may discover my past. To the point that I allowed it to stop me from stepping out in faith into areas to which I knew the Lord was calling me. The enemy had too long won that battle in my life.

If our pasts were put under a microscope, all would be littered with sin and failure. However, if we have run to the Savior and repented and turned away from those, there are amazing promises as in 1 John 1:9; *"If we confess our sins, He is faithful and just to forgive us our sins, and to cleanse us from all unrighteousness"* and Psalm 103:12 *"As far as the east is from the west, So far has He removed our transgressions from us."*

These Scriptures are widely known and loved. Walking fully in these Scriptures is another story. This book will be a great tool in your pursuit of freedom from your past.

My prayer for this book is that it will be used to heal the brokenhearted, to proclaim liberty to the captives, and the opening of the prison to those who are bound. I am going to share with you some of the lessons the Lord has taught and is teaching me in setting me totally free from my past, the fear of it being discovered, or letting it keep me from destiny. The Lord is no Respecter of persons. These Biblical truths are for everyone and will accomplish the same in anyone who applies these to their life.

The message of this book came out of the passage in John 8, where Jesus was brought a woman caught in adultery. As I was studying this story one morning, the Lord spoke to me about what became the title of this book, "Scars Not Stones".

I pray that the Lord will guide you into the truth as you read, and that the truth will make you free.

Donna Williams

1 FIRST THINGS FIRST

John 8:2 - Now early in the morning He came again into the temple, and all the people came to Him; and He sat down and taught them.

The first thing we see in this story is that Jesus was in the temple early one morning. As usual, people gathered to Him and as they did, He taught them. This is such an encouraging scene because it shows us that the Lord is always available to those who draw near to Him as His word promises in James 4:8, *"Draw near to God and He will draw near to you"*.

Let's get the picture here. The Lord is in the temple teaching those who have gathered to Him and while this is happening, the scribes and Pharisees bring into the temple a woman who had been caught in the very act of adultery.

Can you imagine this scenario? It would be the same as on a Sunday morning during the pastor preaching his sermon and a group of people enter boisterously into the church with a person that has been caught in a sin. The mob gives no thought to the fact that the Word of God is being spoken. No thought of their disrespectfulness of the sacred assembly. No care for those people who have gathered to worship the Lord.

My husband and I pastor a church and the thought of this happening during one of our worship services is incomprehensible. But this is exactly what is happening here. The Pharisees and scribes bring this poor lady into the midst of the temple. Can you imagine how she feels?

They state to Jesus that she was "caught in the very act". Did they care enough to at least let her put some clothes on or was she brought in naked? They quote the Law of Moses to Jesus stating that she should be stoned. The Word explains then that they wanted to test Jesus to have something of which to accuse Him and asked Him what He said about the matter.

The scribes and Pharisees had no real concern about maintaining obedience to God's Word here. If so, they would have brought the man who was also caught in the act, because the Law of Moses, which they were quoting, would have required that both the man and the woman caught in the act should have been stoned.

The real issue here was that the Pharisees and scribes hated the fact that Jesus was liked by the people more than they. He performed miracles, signs, and wonders. They felt threatened by Him. He had an authority on Him that made them envious. They were, after all, the Pharisees and the scribes. Who does He think He is?

James 3:16, says *"For where envy and self-seeking exist, confusion and every evil thing are there."*

This is the spirit that was behind the motivation of the Pharisees and scribes. They did not care about the one who was in bondage to sin, the woman, and they wanted to destroy the One who came to set free all those in that bondage. All that mattered to them was that their reputations were elevated even at the cost of others.

It is the same game that Lucifer played when he tried to exalt himself above the Most High. Since we are created in the image of the Most High, the enemy hates us. This is the reason that he is always coming to accuse. He is always coming to kill, steal, and destroy. He always tries to make us question the Word of God.

Remember in the Garden of Eden when he came to Eve? He asked her, "Did God really say?" Or when in the wilderness, he came to tempt Jesus, he tried the same tactic of trying to trip up Jesus when he said to Him, "If You are the Son of God, then do *blank*." The enemy used the Word of God, just not rightly divided. This is what the Pharisees and scribes were doing when they asked Jesus what did He say about what the Word of God said? They were trying to trip Him up so as to have something of which to accuse Him.

In the process of achieving freedom from our past, it is most important what *we* say about what the Word of God says.

The next reading in this John 8 passage is Jesus' response to the scribes and Pharisees. He stoops down and begins writing in the dirt as if He doesn't even hear them. We can learn from the Lord here about how we should deal with the voice of the enemy that tries to condemn us or keep us in guilt and shame about our past.

I love that Jesus did not rashly answer them. He took

His time. Perhaps to listen for the response that the Father would have Him give. This is a great example, also, from which we can learn when we experience being pressured by those that are just trying to trip us up. We can take our time to listen to the Holy Spirit and respond the way that He would have us to, instead of reacting by our flesh to the ill behavior of others toward us. The latter will only lead to further strife instead of the outcome that Jesus achieved.

His response was to answer their question with this statement, *"He who is without sin among you, let him throw a stone at her first."* That was it. Enough said. Nothing more needed. He simply stooped back down and started writing in the dirt. This one simple sentence caused the mob to drop their stones and walk away. Powerful.

The lesson for us here is that the Lord will always give us the right response, and sometimes the best response may be a one statement reply or, perhaps, no response at all.

Once He had silenced the mob, He simply went back to being about His Father's business. He turned to the one caught in sin and offered to her the forgiveness that was His to offer because of the scars that He was going to receive in His hands.

He is the same yesterday, today, yes, and forever. Those scars are still in His hands today making it possible for you and me to do exactly as this lady; to be forgiven of our sin, to be freed from the accusations of the past, and to go and sin no more.

2 THE WORD MADE FLESH

"In the beginning was the Word, and the Word was with God, and the Word was God. He was in the beginning with God. All things were made through Him, and without Him nothing was made that was made. In Him was life, and the life was the light of men. And the light shines in the darkness, and the darkness did not comprehend it." John 1:1-5

"And the Word became flesh and dwelt among us, and we beheld His glory, the glory as of the only begotten of the Father, full of grace and truth." John 1:14

If we are ever going to be freed from our past, we are going to have to start at the beginning of our story in John 8. Jesus was teaching the Word. This is and must always be our starting place. The Word of God.

Jesus is, of course, the incarnate Word of God. This means literally that He is the Word of God in the flesh. Verse 14 in John chapter 1, says that He is full of grace and truth. In John 8:32, it says that we will know the truth and the truth will make us free. Therefore, the only way that we will ever be free from the past is by knowing the truth.

Knowing the truth in this passage means more than knowing about something. The word for 'know' in the original language is a verb. If we think back to our English class from school, we remember that a verb is an action word. It means you actually have to do something. Therefore, I have to know the truth, or another way we can say it to understand the full meaning is that we have to 'know' (verb, action word) or *act on* the truth.

In James 1:22, it says that we must be doers (action) of the Word (truth) and not hearers only or we deceive ourselves. In other words, if I hear the truth that says, *"do not be conformed to this world, but be transformed by the renewing of your mind"* (Romans 12:2) but I never take any steps to renew my mind by studying the Word of God, then I can't be surprised when my mind is full of worry, fear, doubt, and any other thought that is of this world and not from above.

It is the same with being set free from our past. We must study, obey and apply to our lives, every area of His word that promises that our sins are cast as far as the east is from the west, or that He says that He will remember them no more, or that He has pardoned our iniquity.

Pardoned. It is more than just a wonderful sounding word. It is an action that the Lord Himself has bestowed upon those who are guilty, but have thrown themselves on the mercy of His court by repentance.

In the natural world, if one commits an illegal act and is caught, taken to court, and found guilty, they are deserving of the full penalty of the law. However, if the Governor grants a pardon, it means that the person is forgiven the debt, the penalty has been removed, and the offense is removed from the record for all time. It can never legally be brought against that person ever again.

This is what the Lord has done for those of us who have repented of our sin. We acknowledged that we are guilty and deserving of the penalty of the crime, but we threw ourselves on the mercy of the Savior. By

His grace and by His blood the Father then pardons our offence. It can never be held legally against us anymore.

We never forget that we committed the crime and neither does the accuser of the brethren. He loves to remind us and keep us bound by fear that someone else may find out about it.

So many people are silenced and paralyzed by his threats that they haven't stepped out in confidence into the call of God for their lives. If this is you, then in the Name of Jesus, this is your time once and for all to know and act on the truth and finally be free. Free of the fear of someone finding out. Free of the shame of remembering your sin. Free of the guilt that has been pardoned.

The only way this will ever happen in any of our lives is by studying the Word, believing the Word, and applying the Word which means we do what the Word says.

Ephesians 6:17 says that the Word of God is our sword. The Word is our weapon. There is only one reason a person needs a weapon and that is to fight an enemy. Too long we have been unskilled in using our weapon. It is time to train in wielding our weapon.

I am reminded of one of my grandsons who had seen a pirate movie and loved the sword fighting scenes. When he was about 5 years old, he came to visit us one week and I took him to a fencing school where he could learn about sword fighting.

He wasn't in the class very long until he became bored because all he wanted to do was sword fight. He had no desire to learn the correct way to hold the sword or the proper way to stand. He just wanted to play sword fighting. He did not care at all about the clothing he had to wear or the face mask, he just wanted to sword fight.

It is the same with us many times. We just want to quote a couple of Scriptures and presto, we are free. However, we must learn to stand according to the instructions of the Master and properly wield our weapon.

We have been given not only a weapon, but also armor. We must put on the whole armor of God and when we do we will be able to withstand against the schemes of the enemy who wages war against us and tries to keep us in captivity to our past.

Remember at the beginning of our story in John 8. Jesus, who is the Master, went into the temple and taught. As we learn of Him and do things His way, we will know and act on the truth and the truth will cause us to win in the battle from our freedom.

Ephesians 6:10-17 "Finally, my brethren, be strong in the Lord and in the power of His might. Put on the whole armor of God that you may be able to stand against the wiles of the devil. For we do not wrestle against flesh and blood, but against principalities, against powers, against the rulers of the darkness of this age, against spiritual hosts of wickedness in the heavenly places. Therefore take up the whole armor of God that you may be able to withstand in the evil day, and having done all, to stand. Stand therefore, having girded your waist with truth, having put on the breastplate of righteousness, and having shod your feet with the preparation of the gospel of peace; above all, taking the shield of faith with which you will be able to quench all the fiery darts of the wicked one. And take the helmet of salvation, and the sword of the Spirit, which is the word of God;"

3 THAT'S NOT PHARISEE

Matthew 23: 5-8 - "But all their works they do to be
seen by men. They make their phylacteries broad and
enlarge the borders of their garments. They love the
best places at feasts, the best seats in the synagogues,
greetings in the marketplaces, and to be called by men,
'Rabbi, Rabbi.'"

As I began to study about the Pharisees and scribes, it
became obvious that there was one recurring attitude
among them, self-righteous pride. The above Scripture
in Matthew 23 best describes the Pharisees in a way
that is easy to understand. The bottom line about the

Pharisees is that they did everything for appearance. Their heart was not sincere. The "works" that they did were only done for show. This is why they had such a hard time with Jesus. He came as the servant of all. He did not do works for His own glory, but for the glory of His Father.

There are many lessons that we can learn from the behavior of the Pharisees, but one of the most important is that of being judgmental. Webster's definition of judgmental means to judge too quickly and critically. We see the Pharisees doing this all the time with Jesus. He healed the blind man, they were critical because it was the Sabbath. He cast out demons, they were critical and said that He cast out demons by Beelzebub. He ate with the tax collectors and sinners to bring them the Gospel and they were critical because He was hanging out with people with whom they would not associate.

The Pharisee spirit puts high and harsh expectations on everyone but does not hold itself to the same standard and lives exactly opposite of that standard.

Matthew 23:4 - For they bind heavy burdens, hard to bear, and lay them on men's shoulders; but they themselves will not move them with one of their fingers.

When the Pharisee spirit begins to rise up within the Body, great harm follows. Whether you have been hurt by the Pharisee spirit or you have been used by it to hurt others, we must recognize it and not be the receiver or the giver of it.

If we have been hurt by it, we may be easy prey to its enticement to become one that operates in it in an effort to protect ourselves from being hurt by it ever again. We slowly begin to start pointing out others weaknesses to try to elevate ourselves in the eyes of everyone else. We must be on guard to this very sly tactic of the enemy. The Pharisee spirit will harden our hearts so much that we will not recognize that we have become like the very thing that wounded us.

We must forgive those who have treated us with the Pharisee spirit. We must repent to the Lord if we have become those who are behaving under its influence so that we are now operating in it towards others.

I think that it is important that we clarify here that being judgmental is different than discernment. In this present day in which we live, there is a great movement in the world that is permeating the church. It is this statement "you cannot judge me". This is almost always used by people who are living a lifestyle that is practicing sin. The Scripture that is usually used is Matthew 7:1, which says *"Judge not, that you be not judged. For with what judgment you judge, you will be judged; and with the measure you use, it will be measured back to you."* However, in this passage, the context is condemning someone or exacting a sentence upon them for some wrong doing. One of the definitions in the original language is to avenge. In our modern day times it would be the equivalent of a vigilante. One who takes the law into their own hands. In this way, we are not to judge nor are we *THE* Judge, but discerning or 'judging' good and evil is something that we not only can do but must. Look at *Hebrews 5:14, "But solid food belongs to those who are of full age, that is, those who by reason of use have their senses exercised to discern both good and evil."*

Let me give you an example. In our home church, if we have those serving in leadership who begin to engage in behavior that is in direct opposition to the codes of conduct and ethics to which they have submitted, then we as the pastors and the elder team have an obligation under the Lord to address this issue with the person engaged in such activity. For one to behave opposite of those codes is disobedience. Once confronted about the behavior there are two choices, repentance or rebellion. If the offender repents, they are restored to their place of authority; however, if there is not repentance, but a refusal to acknowledge wrong doing, this is rebellion. There must then follow appropriate measures to deal with the wrong behavior.

There is Truth. There is right and wrong. There is good and evil. We can discern or 'judge' these. This is not the same as being judgmental, nor is it the same as in the Matthew 7:1 passage, where we are condemning someone of a wrong they have done.

We must check our hearts. Have we become those who are cold, hard, unloving, critical of others, and unwilling to take the plank out of our own eye? If so, then we must run to the Lord in repentance, asking Him to consume our hearts with His refiner's fire and burn away the dross that we may once again be those that He may send to others as instruments of His love, mercy, and grace. Then we will be those vessels of compassion, not condoning sin but compelling those caught in sin to come to the Savior.

Father, I pray right now for those reading this book who have encountered the Pharisee spirit, whether the recipient of its harm or a pawn it uses to inflict hurt onto others. Deliver Your child right now, in the Name of Jesus. Give us eyes to see, hearts to understand, and feet to run swiftly to You and Your mercy. Without You we can do nothing. Help us become witnesses of Your Truth that sets men free. Start with us so that with the comfort we have received, we will comfort others. In Jesus' Name.

4 CAUGHT IN THE ACT

John 8:3-5 - Then the scribes and Pharisees brought to Him a woman caught in adultery. And when they had set her in the midst, 4 they said to Him, "Teacher, this woman was caught in adultery, in the very act.

Probably most of us can identify with the scene in which this woman in John 8 finds herself. Although our sin may not be the same, getting "caught" is a feeling everyone has most likely experienced at one time or another.

Let's look closely and practically at this story. It's Sunday. The church is full. The preacher is preaching the sermon. You have been caught in the very act of whatever it is that you were doing. A mob, that should have been in church listening to the sermon themselves, catch you in the act.

They grab you and force you to go into the church, in the middle of the message. All heads turn, all eyes are on you, everyone wants to know what is going on. The mob takes you to the front of the church and exposes your sin in front of everyone. All you can do is hang your head in shame. You are, after all, guilty. Surely, the pastor is going to join the band wagon. Surely, he is going to take over the continuation of this parade of your sin.

I am so thankful that the Lord didn't deal with me the way in which the mob wanted. He didn't deny that I had sinned. Indeed, He acknowledge that I had, because He forgave it. He cleansed it. He redeemed it.

He redeemed me. He has redeemed you also if, in fact, you have called upon Him and repented of your sin. Therefore, you have been forgiven and He says to you, "Go and sin no more."

Can you believe that He has forgiven you? Can you receive it? It is easy to believe this about the Lord because He is good and always does good. The hard part comes now in forgiving yourself.

Many years ago, I was attending a women's conference. I was not a guest speaker but had been asked to be a part of the leadership of the conference. One session during worship, I was off to the side, eyes closed, hands lifted, and lost in the Presence of God. All of a sudden with no one near me, I fell to the floor sobbing. As I lay there weeping unto the Lord, He spoke to my heart. "Donna, breathe in deep and tell me what you smell." I was so excited at the possibility of smelling some heavenly aroma. He said to me again, "What do you smell?" Perplexed and somewhat disappointed I answered, "Salt water". He then said to me, "It is the saline of the Holy Spirit and I am irrigating shame out of your life."

I lay there for what seemed like hours more and when I got up, I was free of shame that I didn't even realize had taken root in my life. I understood that this was shame from years and years that had been pushed further down deeper each time something would occur in my life, either by my own doing or the doing of others.

I was free of the shame of having been fondled as a little girl by a family member. I was free of the shame of having been groped by a cousin in elementary school. I was free of the shame of having been molested by a guy in junior high. I was free of the shame of years of promiscuity. I was free of the shame of divorce. I was free of the shame of all the failure in my life for which I had been forgiven.

From that moment on and for the first time in my life as a Believer, I was able to share the testimony of being molested. Until that time, I would never mention it because of the shame that I was unaware had even been there.

I imagine that this is how this woman in John 8 possibly felt. I can identify with her in the area of the shame she must have felt as the mob announced to everyone in the temple about her failure. However, there was One Who approached her differently. He was not shocked or surprised about her failure, indeed, His very conversation with her told her that He was her only hope. And He is our only hope.

I want to encourage you that if you are still haunted by being caught in the act, if you are living under a weight of shame, or if you have just been made aware by the Holy Spirit that you have been living in shame, now is your time. Today is your day to be freed from the burden of shame.

The next obstacle that I am sure our gal in John 8 faced was living with the fear of others finding out about her past sin. I believe that this is the primary area that the enemy uses to hold us hostage and keep us paralyzed so that we won't step out in faith to follow God into the great unknown. That promised land that waits for us. The enemy tells us that we can't go there because it is just a matter of time before people find out. If they find out, it will be the temple scene all over again. It will be easier if you just sit back and stay quiet. Sound familiar?

I want to be a witness to you that the Lord is your Vindicator and He will fight for you.

If your greatest failure, whatever it is, has been repented of, turned from, and is under the Blood and pardoned by the King, then it is inadmissible in the court of the Lord. I am a witness that if there are others that try to bring it up, that the Lord will move on your behalf. Others may try to remind you, may try to destroy you by telling others, but I can confirm and attest to you that Isaiah 54:17, is true when it says, *"No weapon formed against you shall prosper, And every tongue which rises against you in judgment you shall condemn. This is the heritage of the servants of the Lord, and their righteousness is from Me," Says the Lord.*

So, dear one, dare to believe the Lord and step out of the boat. The wind and the waves may become boisterous and scary, but the Lord will never let the righteous be forsaken. That is exactly what, I believe, our John 8 lady did. Why do I believe that? When the Lord asked her where her accusers were after He had silenced them, she referred to Him as 'Lord'. We understand by the Word of God that no one can say that Jesus is Lord except by the Spirit.

Therefore, if she was not saved before this time, I believe she was then. If she had been saved before then and had fallen into sin, then acknowledging Him as Lord shows that she was submitting to His command to go and sin no more.

Do you have failure in your past? Have you repented? Have you turned? Then the Lord says to you, "Where are those accusers of yours? Go and sin no more."

John 8:10-12 When Jesus had raised Himself up and saw no one but the woman, He said to her, "Woman, where are those accusers of yours? Has no one condemned you?" She said, "No one, Lord." And Jesus said to her, "Neither do I condemn you; go and sin no more." Then Jesus spoke to them again, saying, "I am the light of the world. He who follows Me shall not walk in darkness, but have the light of life."

5 WRITINGS IN THE DUST

John 8:5-6 Now Moses, in the law, commanded us that such should be stoned. But what do You say?" This they said, testing Him, that they might have something of which to accuse Him. But Jesus stooped down and wrote on the ground with His finger, as though He did not hear.

Jesus' response to the Pharisees is one of my most favorite parts of this story in John 8, second only to His dealing with the woman. The Pharisees have come to test Jesus once again, of which I am sure He is aware.

He always perceived their thoughts. They were not concerned with the woman's salvation or redemption. They were not concerned with the Word of God being obeyed. They only desired to catch Jesus in some action or teaching for which they could condemn Him in the eyes of all the people.

I love the Lord's response, as He does not engage them on their level. He deals with the heart of the matter, their motives. He uses the opportunity to redeem a daughter who was being used as a pawn in this game the Pharisees were playing.

Jesus doesn't answer initially. He stoops down and begins to write in the ground. Reading this story years ago, I had wondered what He may be writing. I could imagine all sorts of things. Then one year during the Thanksgiving holiday we were visiting my sister-in-law. Some of her husband's side of the family were there as well, including a nephew who was attending seminary.

During the conversation around the table, the topic of this story in John 8 came up. I made the comment that I would love to know what the Lord was writing in the ground.

The nephew begin to share with me a Scripture that he had been studying at seminary that he thought would bring some clarity, and it did. Jeremiah 17:13, says: *"O Lord, the hope of Israel, All who forsake You shall be ashamed." Those who depart from Me shall be* **written in the earth**, *because they have forsaken the Lord, The fountain of living waters."*

Here it was, a scriptural possibility of what the Lord was writing on the ground. Could He, in accordance with the Jeremiah 17:13 scripture, have been writing the names of all those standing there with the stones in their hands ready to stone the woman?

Here the Pharisees stood in their pride trying to trick and test the Lord. Giving no thought that the Hope of

Israel was in their midst. There they stood before the
Lord having departed from His will and His ways.
Therefore, He could have been doing exactly what this
passage proclaimed would happen to those who
depart from and forsake Him. They would be written in
the earth.

So, let's paint the picture. Jesus is teaching in the
temple. This group of Pharisees bring in the woman
and ask Jesus what He says they should do with her. He
stoops down and begins writing on the ground (in the
earth) and doesn't say a word. The Pharisees continue
to ask and finally, Jesus stands up and makes this
statement *"He who is without sin among you, let him
throw a stone at her first."* He then stoops down again
and continues writing on the ground.

The word says, *"Then those who heard it, being
convicted by their conscience, went out one by one,
beginning with the oldest even to the last."* I find it
interesting that the mass exodus of the Pharisees

began with the oldest and ended with the youngest. The oldest one would have been reading the Word the longest and would definitely have known this Scripture reference in Jeremiah.

We can learn from this account this very important fact: the Lord will not only fight for us but He will shut the mouths of those who would come to accuse us. Our part is to sit in quiet confidence and let Him. He knows the best way to deal with them, as we see in this story. It says, *"they were convicted in their conscience"*.

I don't know what your past holds or those who try to hold your past over you. I do know this, if you have repented and turned from those sins and failures then it is under the Blood. It is removed as far as the east is from the west. It has been cast into the sea of forgetfulness. It is remembered no more. This doesn't mean that the Lord has a bad memory. It means that

He has pardoned it and it has be expunged from the record.

That is from the Lord's perspective. The issue is that there are people who may remember. There are people who may try to expose. This is what the enemy will use to bully us into silence. To instill in us a terror that someone may find out or someone else may expose us. I cannot guarantee you that this may not happen, however, I can assure you that if it does that it is not coming from the Lord, even if it is coming through people who claim to be His. He remembers it no more and He, therefore, never reminds us of it either.

I can assure, also, that if someone is using it as a means to harm you or elevate themselves, that the Lord is more than capable of handling the situation. The hard part will be to not try to defend yourself. The flesh always wants to defend. However, what can we say really? We do have a past. We can't deny it; however, if forgiven then it is exactly that: the *past.* We must apply the word to this area of our lives just as the apostle Paul when he said, *"but one thing I do, forgetting those things which are behind and reaching forward to those things which are ahead,"* (Philippians 3:13b). I realize that we will never be able to actually 'forget'; that is not what Paul means here. The word 'forget' here in the original language means to neglect and it is taken from two other words in the Greek. The first means the place or order and the second one means to be hid, to be ignorant of, unaware.

We can conclude then in this context that although the memory will never be gone, we do not have to give it a place or order in our lives. We can let it be hid and choose to not give it any awareness. This will be, at times, a great battle. In these times, we must do what we learned in Chapter 2, put on the whole armor and wield our weapon, the Sword of the Spirit, the Word of God.

The word will always bring about the exact right result at the exact right time. Just as Jesus did for our lady in John 8. Sometimes it may seem strange, like when He stooped down and wrote on the ground. No matter what He does or how He chooses to do it, rest in His way. His way will always be right, even if it just feels that He is simply stooping down, not saying anything and drawing in the dirt.

6 ALONE BUT NOT LONELY

John 8:9b And Jesus was left alone, and the woman standing in the midst.

Jesus was left alone. What an incredible encouragement. Remember that the Pharisees and scribes came to test Him. Trying to trip Him up. However, we saw in the last chapter how He was able to silence them and their consciences were convicted. They then left Jesus alone.

This isn't a picture of no one wanting to be with Jesus so that He was all by Himself. He wasn't rejected by friends or not picked for the team here so that He was alone. This says that He was 'left alone'. The Pharisees' and scribes' schemes were thwarted. They could not triumph over the Lord so they had no choice but to leave Him alone. To not mess with Him anymore.

We live in a suburb of Houston, Texas. The State of Texas has a slogan that was created to combat littering of its highways. The slogan says, "Don't Mess with Texas." This is the message that the Pharisees and scribes received loud and clear on that day, "Don't mess with Jesus".

We see in this passage also that the woman was standing in the midst. I love that she was standing. I would imagine that had I been in her shoes, I would have wanted to crawl into a corner. To get as low and hidden as I could. She comes through this, though, standing on her feet.

49

Jesus won the battle that had come against Him, but the woman was delivered also. Isn't that the same for us? Jesus won the battle against death, hell, and the grave when He went to the cross and then rose again. He won and we are delivered. It is easy to trust this for our initial salvation, but why is it hard to trust when we are in the midst of a situation that seems hopeless? Somehow we act as if we can handle the 'real-life' situations on our own; we will just leave the big, supernatural stuff to God.

Too often we have an idea of how we want things to go or how we want situations to be handled. Since the Lord's ways are not our ways and His thoughts are higher than our thoughts, we don't want to wait on Him. Besides, He might not do it the way that we want. If we are honest with ourselves and the Lord, it comes down to thinking that we know what is best or that we can handle things much better.

I am sure the woman in John 8 thought it very strange that this Teacher stooped down on the ground and started writing. It must have seemed like He wasn't even interested in what would happen to her. I wonder if inside she was hoping that He would rise to her rescue like a knight in shining armor. Instead, He stoops down. This woman was in the very fight for her life and He's drawing? I am sure she had many thoughts of what He should do to deliver her from death and He wasn't doing anything like she thought.

Isn't it the same for us? We have ideas about how the Lord should do something. Ideas about the best way situations should be handled. The danger with this is that almost always, the Lord never does things the way we think, so when we think that He isn't doing anything, we have a crisis of faith. We somehow believe that because He doesn't do it the way that we think it should go, that He doesn't love us, or He doesn't care about how we feel. The enemy then takes the opportunity to reinforce these feelings by reminding us that the Lord isn't doing things the way that we want.

Two things that we must learn here: 1. to trust and 2. to stand.

The Lord has a plan. It is a plan for the redemption of the world. He has a plan for us to be a part of His bigger plan. Everything that comes our way, we must trust that He will work all together for our good. *He will work all together for our good.* We don't have to tell Him *how* to do that. When we make the choice to trust that He is working all out for our good, that will bring a rest to our spirit that is unequalled by the world.

Once we choose to trust then all we have to do is stand. In the Ephesians scripture that we have been looking at about putting on the armor of God, it says, *"Therefore take up the whole armor of God, that you may be able to withstand in the evil day, and having done all, to stand."*

From this we understand that our part in the battle is to put on the armor of God so that we may be able to stand. It does not say to put on the armor that we may be able to speak in defense of ourselves. It says that we may be able to stand.

I am not saying that we won't speak the Word of God, but I am talking about defending ourselves in situations such as our woman in John 8 encountered. Indeed, we must speak the Word of God to the situations in our lives. But we do not wrestle against people, but powers and principalities. We can trust the Lord to defend us against people and we can use our weapon, His Word, against powers and principalities.

This is exactly what happened in John 8. The Lord dealt with the people. The woman was delivered. Jesus was left alone by those trying to trap Him, and the woman was not lonely anymore because she had the Lord on her side.

This same principle will work for us as well. Trust. Stand. The Lord will cause you to be left alone by the enemy, but you will never be lonely because He will never leave you nor forsake you.

Exodus 14:13-14 And Moses said to the people, "Do not be afraid. Stand still, and see the salvation of the Lord, which He will accomplish for you today. For the Egyptians whom you see today, you shall see again no more forever. The Lord will fight for you, and you shall hold your peace."

7 ACCUSATIONS BUT NO CONDEMNATION

John 8:10-11 When Jesus had raised Himself up and saw no one but the woman, He said to her, "Woman, where are those accusers of yours? Has no one condemned you?" She said, "No one, Lord." And Jesus said to her, "Neither do I condemn you; go and sin no more."

This scripture reference starts by stating that Jesus had raised Himself. We know that He had stooped down to write in the dirt. But this reminded me also that Jesus was raised from the dead. Because He was obedient to death, even death on a cross, the Father raised Him again and has given Him the name that is above every name. At that name, every knee will bow and every tongue will confess that He is Lord. All authority has been given to Him. So why do we fear man? The psalmist experienced this as well:

Psalm 56:11 In God I have put my trust; I will not be afraid. What can man do to me?

Psalm 118:6 The Lord is on my side; I will not fear. What can man do to me?

Why do we worry about others finding out about our past? Why do we concern ourselves with the approval of others? Why do we work so hard to keep the past hidden? Why do we not step out in faith in God for fear that the past will be exposed?

I believe the answer lies in the fact that we, better than anyone, know the choices that we made of which we are not proud. We know all the 'gory little details' and the enemy loves to use that to his advantage.

One thing that I have learned is that when the past is under the blood, no one needs the 'gory little details'. Our testimony is not in the 'gory little details', our testimony is of the One Who redeemed and restored us from the 'gory little details'. It is the accuser of the brethren that wants to remind us and expose to others the 'gory little details'. That is exactly the spirit under which the Pharisees were operating in the scenario with the woman in John 8.

This is what keeps us in the prison of fear. Any time the accuser comes, it means that accusations are going to be made. We do not have to worry that accusations may come regarding our past if we have repented and turned from those because the Lord is our Defender. He really will protect us even if the accuser of the brethren does bring accusations.

When the accuser does bring these, the accusation is, most often, filled with a portion of truth and a portion of untruth. Be aware. This is a subtle tactic of the enemy to entice us to try to defend ourselves. Especially because what is being promoted, although it contains a smidgen of truth, the majority is false. Don't fall for this trick. Don't engage in his game. The Lord is our Defender. Let Him defend. He will do a much better job than we ever could.

Besides, it really doesn't matter what people think. They are going to think what they want to regardless of what we would say. It just engages us in activity that distracts from all that the Lord is calling us to be. The Lord knows the truth and we know the truth; that's all the really matters.

In Matthew 5:25, it says *"Agree with your adversary quickly.* This is a great practice to form when the accuser of the brethren comes against us reminding us of our past. Agree with him quickly. When he says "remember when you did this?" or "remember how you didn't do that?" or "you can never be used by God because you are not, or are, or did or didn't, or was or wasn't." Agree. "Yes, I did or didn't, was or wasn't then, but I repented and turned to the Lord. Now I am forgiven and redeemed. I am pardoned and restored." Use your weapon to take the thoughts that he brings captive and bring those to the obedience of the Lord Jesus Christ.

Once we deal with the accuser of the brethren, we must now appropriate the Word of the Lord that says *"There is therefore now no condemnation to those who are in Christ Jesus, who do not walk according to the flesh, but according to the Spirit." Romans 8:1*

What a promise. No condemnation. Webster's definition of condemnation says, "a statement or expression of very strong and definite criticism or disapproval, the act of judicially condemning".

This language speaks in a legal tone. When one commits a crime, is arrested, goes to court and found guilty, what follows next is the sentencing. The judge can then say to the offender, "you have been found guilty; I therefore condemn you to *blank.*"

When we fall into sin, we are guilty and deserving of punishment or condemnation. However, once we are in Christ, there is now no condemnation. No punishment when we repent and turn from our sin and back to the Lord.

I want to clarify here that this doesn't now mean that we can live any way we want to because we are not under condemnation. Sin is serious and there are serious consequences that come with it. Some consequences may never be reversed. A relationship may be severed that never gets restored or some time frame of our life may have been wasted that can never be done over. Serious consequences. However, if we truly turn to the Lord, repent and turn away from our sin, there is forgiveness with Him. He pardons and does not execute condemnation upon us. The really great news is that He can restore the years that the locusts have eaten. Hallelujah!

This area, condemnation, is probably one of the hardest to overcome for people. We can accept that the Lord has forgiven us, but we have a much more difficult time forgiving ourselves. We are disappointed with ourselves and don't believe that we deserve forgiveness.

This is the enemy's breeding ground. He loves to throw the fiery darts at the dart board of our self-disappointment and shame. He doesn't even have to be a great shot because we are already doing a pretty good job ourselves.

If you are swimming in the pool of condemnation after you have repented and turned from the sin and back to the Lord, I am throwing you a life preserver from the Word of God. Grab it and hold on to it.

Declare it over your life as much and as often as you need to. It is found in *Romans 8:1-4,* which says, *There is therefore now no condemnation to those who are in Christ Jesus, who do not walk according to the flesh, but according to the Spirit. For the law of the Spirit of life in Christ Jesus has made me free from the law of sin and death. For what the law could not do in that it was weak through the flesh, God did by sending His own Son in the likeness of sinful flesh, on account of sin: He condemned sin in the flesh, that the righteous requirement of the law might be fulfilled in us who do not walk according to the flesh but according to the Spirit.*

It is time to let condemnation go. There is too much yet for you to be in the Lord. This pool party is over!

Lord, I pray over this dear reader right now. I thank You for allowing them to read this and understand that You are breaking them free from their past and free from the condemnation of it as well. Give them courage to say no to the condemnation and yes to all that You have planned and purposed for them. In Jesus' Name.

8 GO AND SIN NO MORE

John 8:11b "go and sin no more."

OK, I know what you are thinking just reading the title of this chapter. "I might as well throw in the towel now because I can never live up to that." I get it. Hang in there, because as we look more closely at this passage, we will actually find great comfort and encouragement. To do this we have to actually look at the Word as a whole. It is dangerous to take one scripture and set up a thought about what it is saying without looking at the meaning throughout the whole Word.

As I studied this passage, I became encouraged when I understood the meaning behind the phrase, "go and sin no more". 'No more' means literally 'no further.' We must remember here that the woman had been caught in the very act of adultery. When she met the Savior, He extended to her forgiveness and pardon as we understand from His statement, "Neither do I condemn thee".

He is communicating with her that she has met the Savior; the Redeemer; the One who has come to set her free from her sins. Now that she has been made free, she no longer has to be a slave to sin. She no longer has to be held by the power of sin. She is free. He then instructs her to go and sin no more, no further.

He is not saying to her that she must never commit another sin in her entire life or she will then be condemned. This is not consistent with the Word as a whole which states in 1 John 2:1-2: *"My little children, these things I write to you, so that you may not sin. And if anyone sins, we have an Advocate with the Father, Jesus Christ the righteous"* or in 1 John 1:9, *"If we confess our sins, He is faithful and just to forgive us our sins and to cleanse us from all unrighteousness."*

I realize that just reading at face value certain scriptures can be confusing. After many years of studying this area, I want to share an easy way to understand what the Scripture teaches regarding this area. Once we become born again, we are a new creation, old things pass away and all things have become new. We now have a new nature. We no longer have the 'sin nature' reigning in us. Therefore, our spirit has no desire to sin. The problem is that we are still housed in a body of flesh, which has to have its deeds put to death. We can do this only by the Spirit.

The Apostle Paul shares with us in Galatians 5 that the flesh wars with the Spirit and the Spirit against the flesh. During our walk with God we must remember that we are on a journey. When we are born again this is the process of salvation. As we begin our journey to grow in the grace and the knowledge of the Lord Jesus Christ, this is the process of sanctification. Did you notice the word I used here, *process?*

So let's look again. We are born again, our spirit is made alive and we receive a new nature from the Lord. Old things pass away and all has become new. This is our spirit man. Our flesh is not new. It is still flesh. It is contrary to the things of the Spirit. This is why the Lord tells us that if we want to follow Him – a process – we must deny ourselves and take up our cross daily. *Ourselves* here is speaking about the flesh that is contrary to the Spirit.

I explain the process of sanctification this way. It is like a baby learning to walk. We, as the parents, encourage and guide. When they take a step and fall, we don't banish them from the family. We help them up, comfort them if they are crying, and cheer them on to try again.

Proverbs 24:16a - For a righteous man may fall seven times and rise again,

As we walk with the Lord, there may be times that we fall. The Lord is there to forgive us, cleanse us, and help us back up if we run to Him in repentance. He encourages us, then, to continue on the journey.

When we read Scriptures like 1 John 3:9, that says *"Whosoever is born of God doth not commit sin; for his seed remaineth in him: and he cannot sin, because he is born of God." KJV,* without considering the word as a whole, it can cause us to believe the lie of the enemy that says "you will never be free from your past, or you must not really be of God, because you committed sin and it says that you wouldn't do that if you were of God."

The word *commit* in this scripture means at its root, *to practice*. It isn't talking about a weakness that overtakes us so then we make a wrong decision, lose a battle with our flesh and enter into a sin. This speaks of a lifestyle. Therefore, we can understand that when one is born again and has been *born of God,* as the 1 John passage says, that person will not have a lifestyle of or practice sin. It does not mean that we will never sin ever again.

Ecclesiastes 7:20 Indeed, there is not a righteous man on earth who continually does good and who never sins. NASU

This is such good news for those of us who have been born again and have blown it. It was not a lifestyle, it was a fall. So get back up and try again. Falling isn't the real failure. Falling and not getting back up is the real failure. Just as a baby would never become a walking adult if when it fell it never got back up and tried again.

For the sake of balance, I want to look at the other side of this coin. There is a teaching permeating the body today that says that since we are under grace, it doesn't matter what we do or how we live because we are under grace. This has become known as the "hyper grace" message.

This is not in keeping with the whole of the Word of God either. Romans 6:1-3, says *"What shall we say then? Shall we continue in sin that grace may abound? Certainly not! How shall we who died to sin live any longer in it?"*

We understand from this passage that we cannot use the "grace card" as a 'do what I want, when I want, how I want' license. This passage also helps to confirm that it is about lifestyle, as it says that we died to sin and we shall not *live* in it any longer.

Grace isn't an approval to be okay to commit sin because it's covered by grace; indeed, grace frees us from it. Let's look at what Titus 2:11-12 says:

"For the grace of God that brings salvation has appeared to all men, teaching us that, denying ungodliness and worldly lusts, we should live soberly, righteously, and godly in the present age,"

Grace brings salvation, but here it shows us that grace also teaches us to deny ungodliness and worldly lust, then to live soberly, righteously, and godly in the present age. This means we do this now.

We are called to live godly lives. Grace will teach us to do so. We understand, also, that we are in a body of flesh and, in the war between the flesh and the Spirit in our lives, the flesh may win a battle. We must never stop if this happens. We must, in the words of a song, "pick yourself up, dust yourself off, and start all over again."

Never let your past keep you from your present or rob you of your future. Never let the enemy tell you that "you have messed up so badly that it no longer matters, why bother."

The Lord paid too heavy of a price for us to allow the very things that He took the penalty for to be permitted to steal, kill, and destroy His plans and purposes for us. We have to say 'no' to the enemy and 'yes' to God. Deny ourselves, take up our cross, follow Him and He will empower us to 'go and sin no more'.

9 NOW WHAT?

John 8:12 "Then Jesus spoke to them again, saying, "I am the light of the world. He who follows Me shall not walk in darkness, but have the light of life.""

I have studied the account of this story many times over the last two decades. It wasn't until this most recent study that it stood out to me that the above scripture is actually included as a part of this story. In the past I had always concluded the study at the 'go and sin no more' passage, but that is not the end.

What an amazing conclusion to Jesus' conversation with the Pharisees during this episode in the middle of the temple. What an incredible statement for the woman. It is her marching orders, so to speak.

This proclamation says to the woman, "you are now in Me, the Light of the World. You will no longer walk in darkness." This is the same for us. We have the light of life living inside of us. We must walk into the world with that light and share it with others. If they receive it, it will bring them life also.

The greatest tragedy to staying bound by our past is that we do not take the light of life into the world. No wonder the enemy pulls out all of the stops when trying to silence us.

You are valuable to the Lord for the advancement of His kingdom. To see others freed from sin and translated from the kingdom of darkness into the Kingdom of His dear Son. This is the way the Lord has chosen to spread the Good News, through us.

There is a world of people who need a Savior just as we did. The fact that we need a Savior means that we needed to be saved. When one needs to be saved, it means, obviously, that they were in trouble.

We should be unashamed to acknowledge that we were in trouble, but focus on the One Who set us free from that trouble. We need to tell others who are in trouble that He will set them free, also. This is the very purpose the Lord bestows upon each of us when we are saved.

He gives to each of us the ministry of reconciliation as the Word tells us in 2 Corinthians 5:18-21: *"Now all things are of God, who has reconciled us to Himself through Jesus Christ, and has given us the ministry of reconciliation, that is, that God was in Christ reconciling the world to Himself, not imputing their trespasses to them, and has committed to us the word*

of reconciliation. Now then, we are ambassadors for
Christ, as though God were pleading through us: we
implore you on Christ's behalf, be reconciled to God.
For He made Him who knew no sin to be sin for us, that
we might become the righteousness of God in Him."

We all have a ministry. The ministry of reconciliation.
We are all ambassadors of the Lord Jesus Christ. How
incredibly amazing. However, we have to be the ones
to step into that role. The Lord will not force us into it,
but He has given it to us.

I love to think about being an ambassador. Of course,
my only reference to what I know comes from the
movies. I have to trust that someone in Hollywood did
at least a little research into the role of an ambassador.

The ambassador does not reside in their own country.
They move to another country to represent their home
country. The Word tells us that we are not of this
world. It is not our home-country.

The ambassador has control of a specific territory known as the embassy. Everything covered by the embassy whether staff, property, or vehicles, is covered by diplomatic immunity.

Diplomatic immunity meant that the ambassador has special protection from what is required of most people by law. Because Jesus lives in us, we now have immunity to the requirements of the Law when dealing with our sin. Because Jesus took our sin, we are now the righteousness of God in Him if we are born again.

We are ambassadors of the Lord Jesus Christ and we can serve Him in this world by representing Him and His kingdom to others. He is the light of the world. We are the carriers of that light.

Let me encourage you if you have been stuck in the past or paralyzed in your present because of the fear of your past being exposed. If you have repented and returned to the Lord, He has forgiven, He has pardoned and He is re-commissioning you to your post as an ambassador of the Lord Jesus Christ. A carrier of the Light of the Life into the world plagued by darkness.

I prophesy to your dry bones by the wind of the Holy Spirit and say "bones rise up". The Lord says that these bones can live. Now rise up and take your place in the army of God. Get back to your post. Hold your rank and see the Lord perform all His good word that He has spoken over your life. Bones rise up!

Romans 4:20-24 He did not waver at the promise of God through unbelief, but was strengthened in faith, giving glory to God, and being fully convinced that what He had promised He was also able to perform. And therefore "it was accounted to him for righteousness." Now it was not written for his sake alone that it was imputed to him, but also for us.

Jeremiah 33:14-16 'Behold, the days are coming,' says the Lord, 'that I will perform that good thing which I have promised to the house of Israel and to the house of Judah: 'In those days and at that time I will cause to grow up to David a Branch of righteousness; He shall execute judgment and righteousness in the earth. In those days Judah will be saved, And Jerusalem will dwell safely. And this is the name by which she will be called: THE LORD OUR RIGHTEOUSNESS.'

10 TAKING YOUR PLACE

2 Corinthians 10:4-5 - For the weapons of our warfare are not carnal but mighty in God for pulling down strongholds, casting down arguments and every high thing that exalts itself against the knowledge of God, bringing every thought into captivity to the obedience of Christ

If we are ever going to be free from the chains of our past and take our place in the call of God for our lives, there is only one way, as we read earlier, and that is the Word of God applied to our lives through the power of the Holy Spirit.

We can get excited when we hear someone teach on the subject of being freed from our past or even be excited to read a book about it, such as this one. However, if we don't apply these teachings from the Word of God and call on the Holy Spirit to empower us to put to death the deeds of the flesh, we will never truly walk in the liberty that Christ has made available to us. Bought and paid for by His blood.

Therefore, I want to conclude this book with the resources needed to win the fight. You still have to be the one to not just hear it (or read it), but do it; even so I want to leave you with an arsenal with which you can engage the enemy and defeat him. Remember, we need to learn to effectively wield our weapon, the Sword of the Spirit, the Word of God.

At the end of this chapter, I have listed Scriptures that will apply to different areas we face when battling against the enemy and our own flesh regarding freedom from our past and taking our place.

The first place to start is forgiveness. If you have not repented and turned from sin, do that now. If you have done that and have already been forgiven, these Scriptures will remind and encourage you as well in your walk into freedom.

My prayer for you is that you will not only be freed from your past, but that your faith, to believe the Lord to accomplish in and through you and all that He has planned for you for the days ahead, will be strengthened and increased. That you will be so released from the burden of the past that you run with ease the race set before you. That you will comfort others with the comfort you have received, and see them set free from the same chains of their past.

Sharing with them the good news that Jesus has scars not stones in His hands and is waiting to save, deliver, redeem, restore, and release them into His destiny for their lives. That you take your place and finish the course the Lord has laid for you, with all the gusto of Heaven, until that day you hear, "Well done, good and faithful servant." In Jesus' Name. Amen.

Scriptures for Your Arsenal

The scriptures listed below are not an exhaustive list for each topic. All scripture references are in the New King James Version, unless otherwise stated.

Whenever you find yourself engaged in warfare over your past, read these scriptures, meditate on them, and rest in them. His Word will always accomplish what He sends it to do. Do not stop until you are free. Once you are free, do not let the enemy trick you into returning to the bondage ever again. In Jesus' Name!

God's Word

Luke 4:4 - But Jesus answered him, saying, "It is written, 'Man shall not live by bread alone, but by every word of God.'"

John 17:17 - Sanctify them by Your truth. Your word is truth.

John 8:31, 32 - Then Jesus said to those Jews who believed Him, "If you abide in My word, you are My disciples indeed. And you shall know the truth, and the truth shall make you free."

Romans 10:17 - So then faith comes by hearing, and hearing by the word of God.

Hebrews 4:12 - For the word of God is living and powerful, and sharper than any two-edged sword, piercing even to the division of soul and spirit, and of joints and marrow, and is a discerner of the thoughts and intents of the heart.

Isaiah 55:10, 11 - "For as the rain comes down, and the snow from heaven, And do not return there, But water the earth, And make it bring forth and bud, That it may give seed to the sower And bread to the eater, So shall My word be that goes forth from My mouth; It shall not return to Me void, But it shall accomplish what I please, And it shall prosper in the thing for which I sent it.

Psalm 119:9 - How can a young man cleanse his way? By taking heed according to Your word.

Psalm 119:11 - Your word I have hidden in my heart that I might not sin against You.

Psalm 119:105 - Your word is a lamp to my feet and a light to my path.

Forgiveness

2 Chronicles 6:21 - And may You hear the supplications of Your servant and of Your people Israel, when they pray toward this place. Hear from heaven Your dwelling place, and when You hear, forgive.

2 Chronicles 30:9 - For if you return to the Lord, your brethren and your children will be treated with compassion by those who lead them captive, so that they may come back to this land; for the Lord your God is gracious and merciful, and will not turn His face from you if you return to Him."

Jeremiah 31:34b - For I will forgive their iniquity, and their sin I will remember no more."

Matthew 6:12 - And forgive us our debts, As we forgive our debtors.

Matthew 6:14-15 - "For if you forgive men their trespasses, your heavenly Father will also forgive you. But if you do not forgive men their trespasses, neither will your Father forgive your trespasses.

1 John 1:9 - If we confess our sins, He is faithful and just to forgive us our sins and to cleanse us from all unrighteousness.

Pardon

1 Samuel 15:25 - Now therefore, please pardon my sin, and return with me, that I may worship the Lord."

Nehemiah 9:17b - But You are God, Ready to pardon, Gracious and merciful, Slow to anger, Abundant in kindness, and did not forsake them.

Isaiah 55:7 - Let the wicked forsake his way, and the unrighteous man his thoughts; Let him return to the Lord, And He will have mercy on him; And to our God, For He will abundantly pardon.

Jeremiah 33:8,9 - I will cleanse them from all their iniquity by which they have sinned against Me, and I will pardon all their iniquities by which they have sinned and by which they have transgressed against Me. Then it shall be to Me a name of joy, a praise, and an honor before all nations of the earth, who shall hear all the good that I do to them; they shall fear and tremble for all the goodness and all the prosperity that I provide for it.'

Jeremiah 50:20 - In those days and in that time," says the Lord, "The iniquity of Israel shall be sought, but there shall be none; And the sins of Judah, but they shall not be found; for I will pardon those whom I preserve.

Micah 7:18-19 - Who is a God like You, Pardoning iniquity and passing over the transgression of the remnant of His heritage? He does not retain His anger forever, Because He delights in mercy. He will again have compassion on us, and will subdue our iniquities. You will cast all our sins into the depths of the sea.

Restoration

Jeremiah 30:17a - For I will restore health to you and heal you of your wounds,' says the Lord

Joel 2:25, 26 - So I will restore to you the years that the swarming locust has eaten, The crawling locust, the consuming locust, And the chewing locust, My great army which I sent among you.   You shall eat in plenty and be satisfied, and praise the name of the Lord your

God, Who has dealt wondrously with you; and My people shall never be put to shame.

Zechariah 9:12 - Return to the stronghold, you prisoners of hope. Even today I declare that I will restore double to you.

Fear

Psalm 23:4 - Yea, though I walk through the valley of the shadow of death, I will fear no evil; for You are with me; Your rod and Your staff, they comfort me.

Psalm 27:1-3 - The Lord is my light and my salvation; whom shall I fear? The Lord is the strength of my life; of whom shall I be afraid? When the wicked came against me to eat up my flesh, my enemies and foes, They stumbled and fell. Though an army may encamp against me, my heart shall not fear; though war may rise against me, In this I will be confident.

Psalm 56:4 - In God (I will praise His word), In God I have put my trust; I will not fear. What can flesh do to me?

Psalm 78:53 - And He led them on safely, so that they did not fear; but the sea overwhelmed their enemies.

Psalm 118:6 - The Lord is on my side; I will not fear. What can man do to me?

Proverbs 29:25 - The fear of man brings a snare, but whoever trusts in the Lord shall be safe.

Isaiah 41:10 - Fear not, for I am with you; be not dismayed, for I am your God. I will strengthen you, Yes, I will help you, I will uphold you with My righteous right hand.'

Isaiah 41:13-14 - For I, the Lord your God, will hold your right hand, Saying to you, 'Fear not, I will help you.' "Fear not, you worm Jacob, You men of Israel! I will help you," says the Lord and your Redeemer, the Holy One of Israel.

Isaiah 43:1 - But now, thus says the Lord, who created you, O Jacob, And He who formed you, O Israel: "Fear not, for I have redeemed you; I have called you by your name; You are Mine.

Isaiah 44:8 - Do not fear, nor be afraid. Have I not told you from that time, and declared it? You are My witnesses. Is there a God besides Me? Indeed there is no other Rock; I know not one.'"

Isaiah 51:7 - "Listen to Me, you who know righteousness, You people in whose heart is My law: Do not fear the reproach of men, Nor be afraid of their insults.

Isaiah 54:4a - "Do not fear, for you will not be ashamed; neither be disgraced, for you will not be put to shame

Isaiah 54:14-15 - In righteousness you shall be established; you shall be far from oppression, for you shall not fear; and from terror, for it shall not come near you. Indeed they shall surely assemble, but not because of Me. Whoever assembles against you shall fall for your sake.

Jeremiah 30:10 - 'Therefore do not fear, O My servant Jacob,' says the Lord, 'nor be dismayed, O Israel; for behold, I will save you from afar, And your seed from the land of their captivity. Jacob shall return, have rest and be quiet, and no one shall make him afraid.

Luke 12:32 - "Do not fear, little flock, for it is your Father's good pleasure to give you the kingdom.

Romans 8:15 - For you did not receive the spirit of bondage again to fear, but you received the Spirit of adoption by whom we cry out, "Abba, Father."

2 Timothy 1:7 - For God has not given us a spirit of fear, but of power and of love and of a sound mind.

Guilt and Condemnation

Psalm 34:22 - The Lord redeems the soul of His servants, and none of those who trust in Him shall be condemned.

Psalm 51:1 - Have mercy upon me, O God, According to Your lovingkindness; according to the multitude of Your tender mercies, blot out my transgressions.

Romans 8:1 - There is therefore now no condemnation to those who are in Christ Jesus, who do not walk according to the flesh, but according to the Spirit.

Hebrews 10:22 - Let us go right into the presence of God with sincere hearts fully trusting him. For our guilty consciences have been sprinkled with Christ's blood to make us clean, and our bodies have been washed with pure water. NLT

Shame

Isaiah 54:4 - Do not fear, for you will not be ashamed; Neither be disgraced, for you will not be put to shame; For you will forget the shame of your youth

Isaiah 61:7 - Instead of your shame you shall have double honor, and instead of confusion they shall rejoice in their portion. Therefore in their land they shall possess double; Everlasting joy shall be theirs.

Joel 2:26, 27 - You shall eat in plenty and be satisfied, And praise the name of the Lord your God, Who has dealt wondrously with you; and My people shall never be put to shame. Then you shall know that I am in the midst of Israel: I am the Lord your God and there is no other. My people shall never be put to shame.

Romans 9:33 - As it is written: "Behold, I lay in Zion a stumbling stone and rock of offense, and whoever believes on Him will not be put to shame."

Romans 10:11 - For the Scripture says, "Whoever believes on Him will not be put to shame."

1 Peter 2:6 - Therefore it is also contained in the Scripture, "Behold, I lay in Zion a chief cornerstone, elect, precious, and he who believes on Him will by no means be put to shame."

Trust

2 Samuel 22:2-4 - And he said: "The Lord is my rock and my fortress and my deliverer; The God of my strength, in whom I will trust; my shield and the horn of my salvation, my stronghold and my refuge; My Savior, You save me from violence. I will call upon the Lord, who is worthy to be praised; so shall I be saved from my enemies.

2 Samuel 22:31 - As for God, His way is perfect; the word of the Lord is proven; He is a shield to all who trust in Him.

Psalm 5:11 - But let all those rejoice who put their trust in You; Let them ever shout for joy, because You defend them; Let those also who love Your name be joyful in You.

Psalm 17:7 - Show Your marvelous lovingkindness by Your right hand, O You who save those who trust in You from those who rise up against them.

Psalm 20:7 - Some trust in chariots, and some in horses; but we will remember the name of the Lord our God.

Psalm 31:19 - Oh, how great is Your goodness, which You have laid up for those who fear You, Which You have prepared for those who trust in You In the presence of the sons of men!

Psalm 34:22 - The Lord redeems the soul of His servants, and none of those who trust in Him shall be condemned.

Psalm 37:5-6 - Commit your way to the Lord, Trust also in Him, And He shall bring it to pass. He shall bring forth your righteousness as the light, and your justice as the noonday.

Psalm 56:3 - Whenever I am afraid, I will trust in You.

Isaiah 12:2 - Behold, God is my salvation, I will trust and not be afraid; 'For Yah, the Lord, is my strength and song; He also has become my salvation.'"

Victory

1 Corinthians 15:57-58 - But thanks be to God, who gives us the victory through our Lord Jesus Christ. Therefore, my beloved brethren, be steadfast, immovable, always abounding in the work of the Lord, knowing that your labor is not in vain in the Lord.

1 John 5:4-5 - For whatever is born of God overcomes the world. And this is the victory that has overcome the world — our faith. 5 Who is he who overcomes the world, but he who believes that Jesus is the Son of God?

ABOUT THE AUTHOR

Donna Williams is an ordained minister and the co-founder of EPIC Ministries, Inc., with her husband, Jerry Williams. Together they cover churches and are pastors to pastors around the world. Donna is an anointed teacher of the Word and speaks at women's conference in the United States and abroad. When not traveling she co-pastors with her husband, their home church, The FORT, located in Houston, Texas. They live in Fulshear, Texas, which is a suburb of Houston.

CONTACT INFORMATION

For more information, please contact:

EPIC Ministries, Inc.
PO Box 941388
Houston, Texas 77094
281-232-6922 Office 281-232-6208 Fax
www.epicministries.org